√

D0709226

20TH CENTURY ART
1940-60
ART
EMOTION *and* EXPRESSION

Please visit our web site at: www.garethstevens.com
For a free color catalog describing Gareth Stevens' list of high-quality books
and multimedia programs, call 1-800-542-2595 (USA) or 1-800-461-9120 (Canada).
Gareth Stevens Publishing's Fax: (414) 332-3567.

Library of Congress Cataloging-in-Publication Data available upon request from publisher.
Fax (414) 336-0157 for the attention of the Publishing Records Department.

ISBN 0-8368-2851-8

This North American edition first published in 2001 by
Gareth Stevens Publishing
A World Almanac Education Group Company
330 West Olive Street, Suite 100
Milwaukee, WI 53212 USA

Original edition © 2000 by David West Children's Books. First published in Great Britain in 2000 by
Heinemann Library, Halley Court, Jordan Hill, Oxford OX2 8EJ, a division of Reed Educational and
Professional Publishing Limited. This U.S. edition © 2001 by Gareth Stevens, Inc. Additional end
matter © 2001 by Gareth Stevens, Inc.

Picture Research: Brooks Krikler Research
Picture Editor: Carlotta Cooper
Gareth Stevens Editor: Catherine Gardner

Photo Credits:
Abbreviations: (t) top, (m) middle, (b) bottom, (l) left, (r) right

AKG London © Kate Rothko & Christopher Rothko/DACS 2000: cover, page 17.
AKG London: pages 3, 4-5, 6, 10(r), 14(both), 15(b), 22(t), 23(l), 26(b).
Bridgeman Art Library: page 18(l).
Bridgeman Art Library © ADAGP, Paris, and DACS, London, 2000: pages 20(b), 23(r).
Bridgeman Art Library © ARS, New York, and DACS, London, 2000: page 11(t).
Bridgeman Art Library © DACS, London, 2000: page 21(t).
Bridgeman Art Library © William de Kooning Revocable Trust/ARS, New York, and DACS,
    London, 2000: page 15(t).
Bridgeman Art Library © Richard Hamilton 2000: page 29.
Bridgeman Art Library © Jasper Johns/VAGA, New York, and DACS, London, 2000: page 25(t).
Bridgeman Art Library © Estate of David Smith/VAGA, New York, and DACS, London, 2000:
    page 19(l).
Bridgeman Art Library Private Collection: page 22(b).
Corbis: pages 4(t), 8(both), 9(b), 10(l), 12(l, r), 12-13(t), 16(both), 19(r), 20(t), 21(b), 24,
    25(b), 26(t), 27(b), 28(both).
Moderna Museet © Untitled Press, Inc./VAGA, New York, and DACS, London, 2000: 27(t).
Tate Gallery: page 9(t).
Tate Gallery Archive: pages 11(b), 18(r).
Tate Gallery © ADAGP, Paris, and DACS, London, 2000: pages 7, 13.
Tate Gallery © Eduardo Paolozzi 2000. All rights reserved, DACS: page 5(t).

Printed in the United States of America

1 2 3 4 5 6 7 8 9 05 04 03 02 01

20TH CENTURY ART

1940-60

EMOTION and EXPRESSION

Jackie Gaff

Gareth Stevens Publishing

A WORLD ALMANAC EDUCATION GROUP COMPANY

CONTENTS

World War II came to an abrupt end in 1945, when atomic bombs were dropped on the Japanese cities of Hiroshima and Nagasaki. More than 100,000 Japanese civilians were killed by the explosions, and many more died later from radiation sickness. Worldwide, about 15 million soldiers and 50 million civilians were killed during the war. In the next decades, wars raged in Korea, Vietnam, the Middle East, and Africa.

TIME OF TENSION

At the dawn of the 1940s, the world was at war. Even after World War II ended in 1945, the peace was fragile. The United States and the Soviet Union began to build up nuclear weapons and seek military and economic allies around the world. Although neither fought each other directly, a state of hostile tension known as the Cold War existed between these two superpowers for the next forty years.

In the shadow of the Holocaust and the atomic bomb, the dominant mood of the 1940s was disillusionment — a loss of faith in everything from systems of government to the methods and purposes of creativity. Few artists turned outward to society, as they had done after World War I, criticizing it or contributing ideas for change. Instead, many artists turned inward to their deepest thoughts and feelings for new ways to express their beliefs about the meaning of art and life.

Pop Art pictures exploded onto the art scene in the mid-to-late 1950s. They marked a shift in direction for the art world. The focus moved away from the artist's personal feelings and returned to social comment and celebration.

World War II fueled the American economy and launched the United States on the greatest growth period in its history. During these years, New York began to replace Paris as the capital of the art world.

ALBERTO GIACOMETTI

For some people, the skeleton-thin figures of Swiss sculptor Alberto Giacometti (1901–1966) brought to mind the starved victims of wartime concentration camps and symbolized the horror and suffering of World War II. For others, these fragile figures, which seemed to fade away into nothingness, expressed existentialist ideas about the nature of human existence.

MAN POINTING
ALBERTO GIACOMETTI, 1947

This delicate sculpture was among the first of the tall, thin figures for which Giacometti became famous. As one of his larger pieces, it stood almost 6 feet (1.8 meters) tall. It was different from his work during the war years, when his experience of sculpting had been disturbing and bizarre. "Wanting to create from memory what I have seen," he wrote about this period, "to my terror, the sculptures became smaller and smaller. They had a likeness only when they were small, yet their dimensions revolted me, and tirelessly I began again, only to end several months later at the same point." All of Giacometti's work from the early 1940s was only about 4 inches (10 cm) tall — not much bigger than a finger!

THREE WALKING MEN, *1948*
Even when Giacometti (left) sculpted groups the individual figures did not seem to notice one another, which reinforced the sense of loneliness that many people saw in his work

6

STRUGGLING TO CREATE
Giacometti worried more about what he was trying to do than about what other people thought about his work. He was trying to re-create exactly what he saw. "I know that it is utterly impossible for me to model, paint or draw a head, for instance, as I see it and yet this is the only thing I am attempting to do . . ." he said. "I do not know whether I work in order to make something, or in order to know why I cannot make what I would like to make." He was never satisfied with his work and constantly destroyed it and started over.

SCULPTING THE FIGURE
Giacometti was one of many artists who concentrated on representational, or figurative, work during this period. Other sculptors who worked in this style were America's Leonard Baskin (*b.* 1922); Britain's Reg Butler (1913–1981), Elisabeth Frink (1930–1993), and Henry Moore (1898–1986); France's Germaine Richier (1904–1959); and Italy's Marino Marini (1901–1980) and Giacomo Manzù (1908–1991).

FRANCIS BACON

Another artist whose work seemed to express the postwar mood of gloom and doom was the great Irish-born painter Francis Bacon (1909–1992). When his *Three Studies for Figures at the Base of a Crucifixion* was first exhibited in London in 1945, it caused such a stir that Bacon instantly became the most talked-about artist in Britain.

A POUND OF FLESH

Bacon used distorted human faces and bodies as his subjects. Bodies were twisted into unnatural, torturous positions. Heads screamed in agony. Skin and flesh dissolved and dripped from boneless forms. Usually the subject was alone and sometimes imprisoned within bars or cages. Backgrounds were often red or black, the colors of blood and death.

8

ART AT WAR

During World War II, many leading artists served as official war artists whose job was to record the events of the war. Photography also was becoming more important through the efforts of people like American Lee Miller (1907–1977). Her images of Nazi concentration camps helped show the horror of the Holocaust.

Miller studied painting in Paris, but by the early 1930s, she was gaining fame as a photographer.

MEATY SUBJECT MATTER

Bacon's vision centered on the cruelty of life. "When you go into a butcher's shop and see how beautiful meat can be and then you think about it, you can think of the whole horror of life — of one thing living off another," he said.

Other leading representational painters included Graham Sutherland (1903–1980, shown with his 1954 portrait of Winston Churchill) and Lucian Freud (b. 1922) of Britain; Larry Rivers (b. 1923) of the United States; Arthur Boyd (1920–1999) of Australia; and Balthus (b. 1908) of France

THREE STUDIES FOR FIGURES AT THE BASE OF A CRUCIFIXION

FRANCIS BACON, 1944 (*right-hand panel*)

In each of the three panels that make up this nightmarish vision, a monster struggles in torment, trapped in a boxlike room. In this panel, a head has changed into a large, screaming mouth. Bacon said that the panels were sketches for the three Furies, the terrible goddesses of revenge in ancient Greek and Roman mythology.

Bacon (below), *who did not believe in God, thought the crucifixion showed how savage humans could be.*

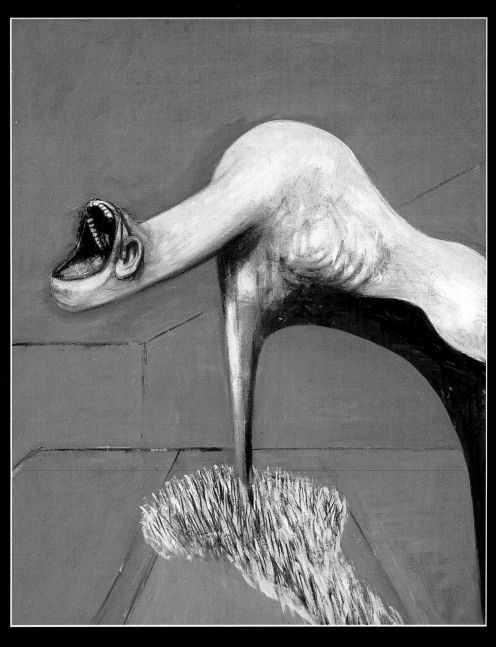

THE SHOCKING TRUTH

Bacon intended not only to shock the people who looked at his paintings, but also to alter their sense of the world. He wanted his art to echo within their deepest selves and disturb "the whole life cycle within a person." About most art, he said, "your eye just flows over. It may be charming or nice, but it doesn't change you."

JACKSON POLLOCK

After the war, European artists such as Giacometti and Bacon continued to have significant influence. The major new art movement, however, came from the United States. It was led by American painter Jackson Pollock (1912–1956).

PAINTING IN ACTION

In 1947, Pollock began experimenting with a completely different way of painting. He took his canvas off his easel and laid it on the floor. Then, instead of brushing on paint, he dripped, flicked, and poured it on, using sticks, trowels, knives, and even turkey basters. Moving around and sometimes right over the canvas, Pollock worked with his whole body. By plunging himself into the act of creating his paintings, he believed he could express the deepest levels of his being.

Pollock said jazz was "the only other really creative thing" happening in the United States. Pollock's painting style was as improvisational as the bebop jazz of musicians like Charlie Parker (above).

PLUMBING THE DEPTHS

In search of a more personal form of expression, Pollock and many other artists were influenced by the theories of Swiss psychiatrist Carl Jung (1875–1961). Jung expanded earlier ideas about the personal unconscious and believed each human is born with memories of a shared, ancestral history. He called these memories "archetypes" and believed that they were revealed through myths and symbols.

Jung believed that art was an important way to keep the myths and symbols of the collective unconscious alive.

THE ART OF EMOTION

Pollock was one of many American artists who explored free, unplanned ways of using paint to express powerful ideas and feelings. This art was abstract, meaning it did not show real objects, and it was expressive, or showed strong emotions. As a result, the movement was called Abstract Expressionism. Pollock did not invent the drip-and-splash technique by himself, or the art movement for that matter, but he "broke the ice," said another Abstract Expressionist, Willem de Kooning (1904–1997).

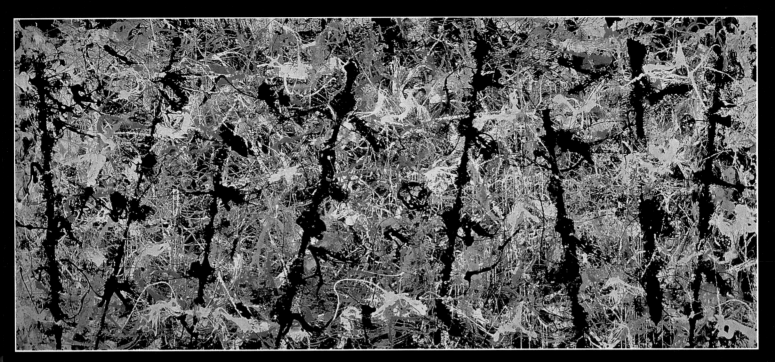

BLUE POLES, NUMBER II
JACKSON POLLOCK, 1952

Instead of painting with just his arm, Pollock used his whole body. He danced around the canvas and made huge sweeping gestures to splatter and splash paint on it. He wanted the rhythmic swirls on his huge canvases to be experienced, not analyzed. Viewers "should not look *for*," Pollock explained, "but look passively — and try to receive what the painting has to offer."

Pollock may have lost himself in the creative act for much of the time, and his application of paint may look hit-and-miss, but his art was not created this way because of luck. "When I am painting I have a general notion as to what I am about," he said. "I can control the flow of paint; there is no accident." *Blue Poles* was one of Pollock's last great works. He died in 1956 in a car accident.

Jackson Pollock (above left) *was a leader in the Abstract Expressionism movement.*

BORN IN THE USA

Abstract Expressionism was the first distinctly new art movement to appear in the United States and have international impact. One of the chief influences on Abstract Expressionism was Surrealism, an art movement born in Europe during the 1920s. Surrealist writers and artists explored the unconscious mind and the world of dreams.

The New York skyline was a welcome sight to the lucky few who managed to escape the war in Europe.

SHIFTING SANDS

Another influence on Abstract Expressionism was the art of Native North Americans. For example, Jackson Pollock's drip-and-splash technique was partly inspired by Navajo sand paintings. Navajos create these paintings by dribbling colored sand through their fingers.

Sand paintings are freehand works done from memory.

DRAWING ON THE UNCONSCIOUS

During World War II, several Surrealists fled Europe to New York, including French poet André Breton (1896–1966), the movement's founder; German artists Max Ernst (1891–1976); and Spaniard Salvador Dalí (1904–1989). American avant-garde was less interested in Dalí's dream imagery than in Ernst's automatism. Automatism was a kind of doodling in which ideas and images are allowed to develop freely from the unconscious. Surrealists tended to use automatism to get ideas for their work, while Abstract Expressionists such as Pollock used it as the spontaneous creation of an entire painting.

After the outbreak of World War II, Max Ernst (left) was imprisoned in France. He escaped to the United States in 1941. This photo shows him being interviewed by an immigration official upon his arrival in New York.

NEW YORK, NEW YORK

Until World War II, Western art was dominated by European artists. Although new movements might have been partly inspired by other influences, avant-garde art had developed in Europe. As the Nazis tightened their grip on Europe, many leading artists sought safety in the United States. Their departure and the birth of Abstract Expressionism shifted the focus of avant-garde art. New York began to replace Paris as the international capital of art.

WATERFALL
ARSHILE GORKY, 1943

American artist Arshile Gorky (1904–1948) is often described as the last of the great Surrealists and the first of the Abstract Expressionists. Armenian-born Gorky arrived in the United States in 1920. For the next two decades, he experimented with Cubism, geometric abstraction, and biomorphic abstraction. In the 1940s, Gorky found his own distinctive style. For images, he drew upon his childhood memories along with his deepest thoughts and desires. Surrealism inspired his use of dreamy, free-flowing color and line. *Waterfall* appears abstract yet evokes a stream plunging through rocks surrounded by trees and greenery. Gorky's work shows the spontaneity that would soon be associated with Abstract Expressionism.

13

ACTION PAINTING

Abstract Expressionists preferred to call themselves the New York School. Although their paintings were as different as their personalities, two distinct styles had developed by the 1950s.

ARTISTS IN ACTION

In the work of some artists, including Pollock, the painter's actions, or gestures, were the main focus. This style is known as Action Painting. Other Americans who used this style were Franz Kline (1910–1962), Lee Krasner (1908–1984), Robert Motherwell (1915–1991), and Dutch-born Willem de Kooning (1904–1997). These painters developed individual techniques. Kline and Motherwell mainly used black paint, sweeping it onto white canvases with huge, expressive brushstrokes.

This rather surreal photograph of Peggy Guggenheim was taken in Venice in 1951.

WOMAN OF MEANS

American art patron and collector Peggy Guggenheim (1898–1979), who was married to Surrealist Max Ernst, supported avant-garde art and furthered the careers of the Abstract Expressionists. She lived in Europe for most of her life but spent the war years in New York.

AMBIGUITIES OF STYLE

Not all Abstract Expressionists attempted or even wanted to work as directly from the unconscious as Pollock did, and not all of them created abstract works — at least not all of the time. Pollock returned to representational art toward the end of his life, while de Kooning moved freely between abstract and representational art throughout his life.

Actress Marilyn Monroe (1926–1962), one of the most popular pin-ups of the 1950s, is one of the most idolized women of all time.

14

MARILYN MONROE
WILLEM DE KOONING, 1954

De Kooning began his *Woman* series in the early 1950s. In these paintings, he used wild, slashing brushstrokes to depict images of women. The images in his earliest works had exaggerated features and looked very aggressive. By 1954, when de Kooning painted *Marilyn Monroe*, the images had a softer look.

Talking about his Woman *series in the 1960s, de Kooning* (below) *said, "I think it had to do with the idea of the idol, the oracle, and, above all, the hilariousness of it."*

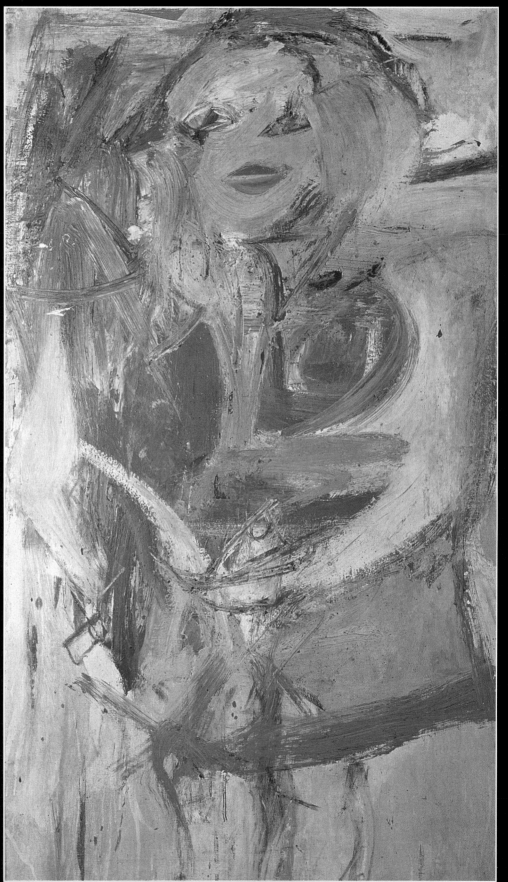

15

COLOR FIELD PAINTING

Instead of using Action Painting, some Abstract Expressionists flooded their canvases with large areas of color. This style became known as Color Field Painting. In the United States, pioneers in this style included Barnett Newman (1905–1970), Ad Reinhardt (1913–1967), Clyfford Still (1904–1980), and Russian-born Mark Rothko (1903–1970).

VARIATIONS ON A THEME

These artists all created totally abstract paintings, but they used different techniques. Most of Newman's canvases were monochrome (painted in a single color), except for one or more vertical stripes, which he called "zips." Rothko, on the other hand, painted hazy, rectangular, cloud-like forms, which seemed to vibrate and drift above the canvas.

LARGE AS LIFE

Size was important to all Abstract Expressionists. Many of their paintings were bigger than large windows, and some were wall-sized. They were supposed to be viewed from close by. These artists believed that only when viewers were "surrounded" could they begin to share in the artist's experience and feel responses of their own.

"To paint a small picture is to place yourself outside your experience…" said Rothko. "However you paint the larger picture, you are in it."

CASH BENEFITS

One reason New York became the center of avant-garde art was the financial support given to artists by private patrons and public organizations. In 1958, for example, Rothko was asked to paint a series of murals for the restaurant in the city's new Seagram Building. Rothko, however, eventually gave the murals to London's Tate Gallery, probably because he felt a busy restaurant wasn't the most spiritual place in which to experience his art.

New York's Seagram Building soars to a height of 525 feet (160 m).

16

WHITE CLOUD OVER PURPLE
MARK ROTHKO, 1957

Although abstract, Rothko's paintings do have subjects. "There is no such thing as good painting about nothing," he said. Like other Abstract Expressionists, Rothko believed in the potential of abstract art to express deep personal and universal truths. "I'm not interested in the relationship of color or form or anything else," he said. "I'm interested only in expressing basic human emotions — tragedy, ecstasy, doom and so on . . . The people who weep before my pictures are having the same religious experience as I had when I painted them."

AMERICAN SCULPTURE

The outstanding American sculptor during the postwar period and, many believe, the most important American sculptor of the 20th century was David Smith (1906–1965).

SURPRISING RESULTS

Smith was a close friend of de Kooning and other Abstract Expressionist painters, sharing many of their beliefs, particularly in Surrealism. He created his sculptures quickly and freely. "I do not work with a conscious and specific conviction about a piece of sculpture . . ." he explained. "It should be a celebration, one of surprise, not one rehearsed."

ARTISTIC INSPIRATION

Smith began working with welded metal in the 1930s, after he saw pictures of welded sculptures by Spaniards Pablo Picasso (1881–1973) and Julio González (1876–1942), the first modern artists to make them. Later, Smith inspired the abstract metal sculptures of one of the leading British artists of the 1960s, Anthony Caro (*b.* 1924).

BOX OF TRICKS
Another influential American sculptor of the period was Joseph Cornell (1903–1972), one of the pioneers of "assemblage" art made from found objects. Cornell's sculptures were a very personal and magical combination of memory and imagination. He searched junk shops and flea markets for objects that he then arranged with maps, photographs, and his own souvenirs in small wooden boxes.

NIGHT SONGS, *Joseph Cornell, c. 1953*

CUBI XIX
DAVID SMITH, 1964

Smith learned to work with metal by building cars in the mid-1920s and locomotives during World War II. His artwork went through many stages. In the late 1930s, he began using found objects, such as industrial tools. During the early 1940s, he experimented with biomorphic abstraction. He painted some sculptures in bright colors and designed others to rust. The mirrorlike stainless steel surfaces of his geometric *Cubi* sculptures reflected sunlight and color. Smith series of *Cubi* sculptures was his last great achievement. He was killed in 1965 in a truck accident.

"Metal itself possesses little art history, Smith said. *"What associations it possesses are those of this century: power, structure, movement, progress, suspension, destruction, brutality."*

CREATIVE EXAMPLES

Other leading American sculptors of the period included Isamu Noguchi (1904–1988) and Alexander Calder (1898–1976), and Russian-born artists Naum Gabo (1890–1977) and Louise Nevelson (1899–1988). Noguchi is best known for stone-carvings of biomorphic abstract forms. Calder and Gabo also made abstract sculptures, and in the 1920s and 1930s, they pioneered kinetic art, which is art that includes movement.

Louise Nevelson was another assemblage pioneer. In the late 1950s, she began making the wall-sized abstract sculptures for which she became famous. She filled shallow box shapes with wooden found objects, from toilet seats to chair legs. Then, she sprayed the entire assemblage with black paint.

JEAN DUBUFFET

Outside of the United States, artists also searched for more expressive and spontaneous forms of creativity. One of the most experimental European artists was Jean Dubuffet (1901–1985) of France.

LA CALIPETTE
JEAN DUBUFFET, 1961

Dubuffet's style was deliberately like that of a young child. Flat, simplified people, dogs, and cars bustle along a wobbly street, against a backdrop of colorful graffiti.

Dubuffet, a former wine merchant, didn't work as an artist full time until 1942.

20

THE EYES OF A CHILD

Dubuffet tried to reinvent art by looking at the world with fresh eyes, uncluttered by history or tradition. Influenced by Surrealism, he admired the simplicity, spontaneity, and directness of graffiti and of art created by children and others outside the professional art world. As a way of describing this kind of art, he invented the term *Art Brut,* which is French for "raw" or "rough art." Dubuffet set up a group to collect and study Art Brut, which is also widely known as Outside Art. "There is only one way to paint well," Dubuffet said, "while there are a thousand ways to paint badly: they are what I'm curious about; it's from them that I expect something new, that I hope for revelations."

CHILD III, *Karel Appel, 1951*
Dutch artist Karel Appel (b. 1921) shared Dubuffet's interest in children's art. "You have to learn it all," he said, "then forget it and start again like a child."

21

WRITING ON THE WALL

Drawings made on rocks or walls, called graffiti, date back to ancient times. However, only in the 20th century have people begun to think of graffiti as art and not just vandalism. Led by Americans Keith Haring (1958–1990) and Jean-Michel Basquiat (1960–1988), graffiti peaked in the 1980s.

In 1986, Haring opened a shop to sell T-shirts and other items that were printed with his artwork.

STREET MATERIALS

Dubuffet experimented with materials and with ways of seeing. In 1946, he began to copy the texture of the walls on which graffiti is found. He built up a surface from substances such as plaster and putty, then scratched into it. Throughout his life, he was fascinated by materials. He made collages from butterfly wings, leaves, and flowers, and sculptures from coal, tree roots, driftwood, and painted metal.

ART MATTERS

In the postwar years, artists from many countries were, like Dubuffet, exploring the expressive qualities both of painting and of the materials, or the matter, of art.

PAINT AND PASTE

French artist Jean Fautrier (1898–1964), for example, built his paintings from layers of a thick mixture of cement, plaster, and paint. The roughly formed faces of his *Hostage* series (begun in 1943) were inspired by wartime experiences that suggest death, decay, and horror. Spaniard Antoni Tàpies (*b.* 1923) built richly textured paintings from found materials, such as string, rags, and cardboard, and paint thickened with sand, marble dust, and other substances.

Italian Alberto Burri (1915–1995) worked with coarse fabric and other found materials.

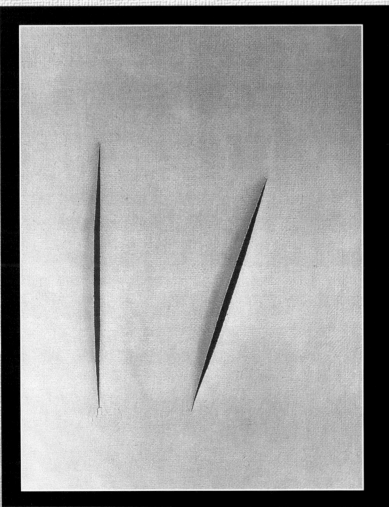

SPATIAL CONCEPT
LUCIO FONTANA, 1959

Argentinian-born Italian Lucio Fontana (1899–1968) launched his Spatialism movement in the late 1940s, calling for a new art for a new age. Among other things, he wanted to remove traditional perspective — that is, the illusion of depth or space — in painting. In 1949, he introduced actual space into his work by punching holes into his paintings. Nine years later, he created the slashed, monochrome canvases, such as *Spatial Concept*, for which he is best known. Fontana wanted to join color and shape with sound, movement, time, and space. He claimed that "a new art will be possible only with light and television." In his spatial environments, he was one of the first artists to use neon lighting to project color and shape into real, three-dimensional space.

SCRIBBLES AND DRIBBLES

Other artists were more interested in the act of painting than in the materials. Gestural and expressive, their style was similar to American Action Painting. However, in the early years, it developed independently of events in the United States. By the mid-1940s, for example, paint squiggles and expressive brushstrokes were being used in a free, unplanned way by German-born artist Wols (1913–1951). Other gestural painters included Pierre Soulages (*b*. 1919) and Georges Mathieu (*b*. 1921) of France, German-born Hans Hartung (1904–1989), and Canadian-born Jean-Paul Riopelle (*b*. 1923).

Tàpies and other postwar artists attacked the traditions of fine art by using unusual materials.

T57-13E
HANS HARTUNG, 1957

Hartung began painting abstracts in 1922, when he was only seventeen years old, and had developed his elegant, gestural style by the late 1930s. His work may appear spontaneously expressive, but he believed in planning and thought. He said that the artist "must try to preserve in the performance, the freshness, directness and spontaneity characteristic of improvisation." Although born in Germany, Hartung spent most of his life in France and became a French citizen in 1946. Instead of titles, he gave his paintings "T" numbers, from the French word *toile*, meaning "canvas."

JASPER JOHNS

In the United States, a reaction against the soul-searching of Abstract Expressionism began in the mid-1950s. A young American artist, Jasper Johns (*b.* 1930), was among those who led the change.

AMERICAN DREAM

In 1955, when he was twenty-five years old, Johns dreamed of painting a large American flag. "The next morning," he said, "I went out and bought the materials to begin it." The result was striking. Unlike Surrealist or Abstract Expressionist dream-inspired artwork, it did not draw on the world of the unconscious. Except for its heavily textured surface, the painting Johns made was almost an exact copy of a real American flag.

Johns drew inspiration from the real world. He made paintings of everyday objects and symbols, such as letters of the alphabet and numbers.

24

THREE FLAGS
JASPER JOHNS, 1958

Johns's 1955 painting of the American flag was the first of a series that included a set of three canvases. He also created *Target*, a series of paintings with rings like those on a shooting target, and made small sculptures of everyday objects, such as beer cans and light bulbs. For Johns, these "found images," or images that are not invented by the artist because they already exist, made his art less personal and more objective. "Using the design of the American flag took care of a great deal for me because I didn't have to design it," he said. "So I went on to similar things like targets — things the mind already knows."

FLAUNTING THE FLAG

Johns wanted to move away from the subjectivity, which is based on personal feelings, of avant-garde American art and make something less emotional and more objective. His work was not obviously about himself, the artist, but about an object, the flag. At the same time, Johns also raised all sorts of complex questions about the meaning of art, the meaning of objects in the real world, and the relationships between them. After all, Johns had not chosen any old object; he had chosen the symbol of U.S. national and cultural identity.

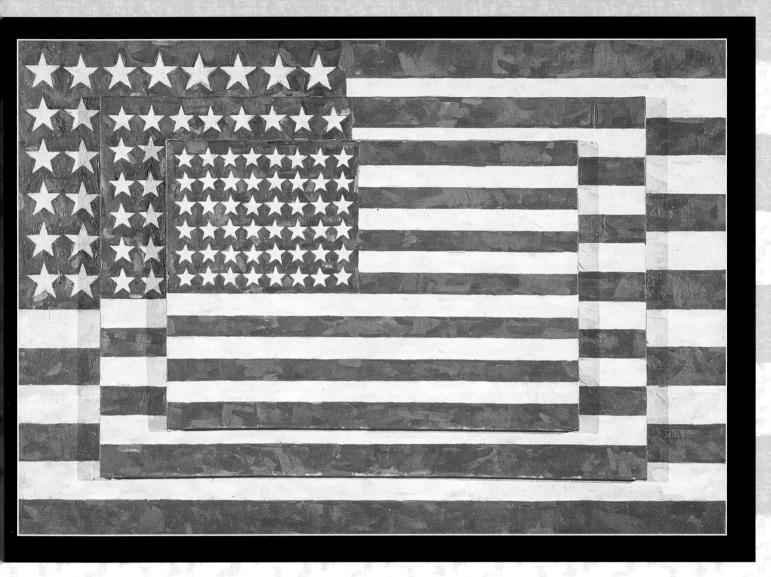

Italian-born American Leo Castelli (1907–1999), who was one of the most influential art dealers of the 20th century, launched Johns's career with an exhibition in 1958.

OBJECT LESSON

The paintings by Johns highlighted the powerful messages that objects and images can communicate. For example, when viewers look at a painting of the American flag, they think about the flag's symbolic meaning. At the same time, however, Johns turned the flag into a flat, painted pattern. In this way, he stripped it of the symbolic and emotional messages that it would have had if it was being held by a soldier in battle or an athlete at the Olympics. On top of all this, his work was also both a painting and a flag. He had bridged the gap between representation, or art, and object, or the real world.

ROBERT RAUSCHENBERG

Johns was not the only artist to react against Abstract Expressionism. His friend, American artist Robert Rauschenberg (*b.* 1925), was just as rebellious and was an equal influence for change.

ROUGH AND READY

If Johns was interested in the found image, his friend was fascinated by the found object. In the mid-1950s, Rauschenberg began to create collages of found objects, often using junk he had picked up on the streets around his New York home. This was not a new technique. Although Rauschenberg called his works "combines," they were actually a form of the assemblage practiced by sculptors like Cornell.

A close friend of Rauschenberg and Johns, Cage (above) greatly influenced their ideas.

MUSICAL GURU

American avant-garde composer John Cage (1912–1992) was an influential figure on the postwar art scene. Cage opposed subjectivity. "There is no room for emotion in a work of art," he said. He valued luck and the everyday, and he thought any sound or noise was music. In his *4' 33"* (1952), for example, the performer sat silently at the piano while the audience listened to sounds in the concert hall or from outside.

CHANCE, NOT CHOICE

While Cornell filled his art with personal connections, Rauschenberg made his combines impersonal, using available items, instead of hunting down specific objects. Like Johns, he wanted to abandon the subjectivity of Abstract Expressionism. "I don't mess around with my subconscious," he said. "I try to keep wide awake. Painting is always strongest when . . . it appears as a fact, or an inevitability, as opposed to a souvenir or arrangement."

French-born American Marcel Duchamp (1887–1968) was a leader of the anti-art movement, Dada, and invented ready-mades (real life objects framed as art). His work inspired Johns and Rauschenberg.

MONOGRAM
ROBERT RAUSCHENBERG, 1955–1959

With its stuffed angora goat and car tire, *Monogram* was Rauschenberg's most famous combine. Others included *Bed* (1955), made from bedclothes splattered with paint, toothpaste, and nail polish, and *Canyon* (1959), which featured a stuffed eagle. Rauschenberg was hugely experimental and soon stopped making combines and moved on to other ideas, including dance and performance art. In *Pelican* (1963), Rauschenberg performed at a roller-skating rink and wore roller skates and a huge, sail-like parachute. He dedicated this work to the pioneers of powered flight, the Wright brothers.

"Painting relates to both art and life," said Rauschenberg. "Neither can be made. (I try to act in that gap between the two.)"

BIRTH OF POP

Pop is short for popular, as in popular culture. In their use of everyday images and objects, Rauschenberg and Johns were godfathers to the American Pop Art movement of the 1960s. Across the Atlantic in Britain, a separate Pop Art movement developed in the 1950s.

MESSAGES FOR THE MASSES

British Pop Art grew out of meetings, beginning in 1952, at London's Institute of Contemporary Arts (ICA). A small group of artists, art critics, and architects met to discuss the images and impact of the mass media and the new age of consumer goods.

LUXURY LIFESTYLES

European economies recovered slowly in the years after the war, and people did not have enough money to afford luxuries until the mid-1950s. The American economy was booming, however, and the ICA group was fascinated by the glossy, colorful lifestyle shown in the American movies, television programs, comics, magazines, and advertisements that were flooding into Britain.

The Whitechapel Art Gallery opened in London's East End in 1900.

POPULAR PICTURES

London's Whitechapel Art Gallery housed a 1956 exhibit, organized by the ICA group, on the new popular culture. Called "This is Tomorrow," it included Hamilton's ground-breaking Pop collage *Just What Is It . . . ?*

PIONEERS OF POP

Eduardo Paolozzi (*b.* 1924) and Richard Hamilton (*b.* 1922) started British Pop Art. In 1957, Hamilton described Pop Art as "popular, transient, expendable, low-cost, mass-produced, young, witty, sexy, gimmicky, glamorous, and Big Business."

Invented in the 1920s but not widely available until after World War II, TV was a powerful tool for reaching large audiences.

JUST WHAT IS IT THAT MAKES TODAY'S HOMES SO DIFFERENT, SO APPEALING?

Richard Hamilton, 1956

The answer to Hamilton's question was everything from a new Hoover vacuum cleaner to a new, muscular body. Was he serious? No, of course not! Hamilton was making a joking but critical comment about consumerism. Hamilton's picture, a collage of advertising images, was one of the first Pop Art works. It even includes the word "pop" on the large lollipop carried by Hamilton's muscle-bound "hero."

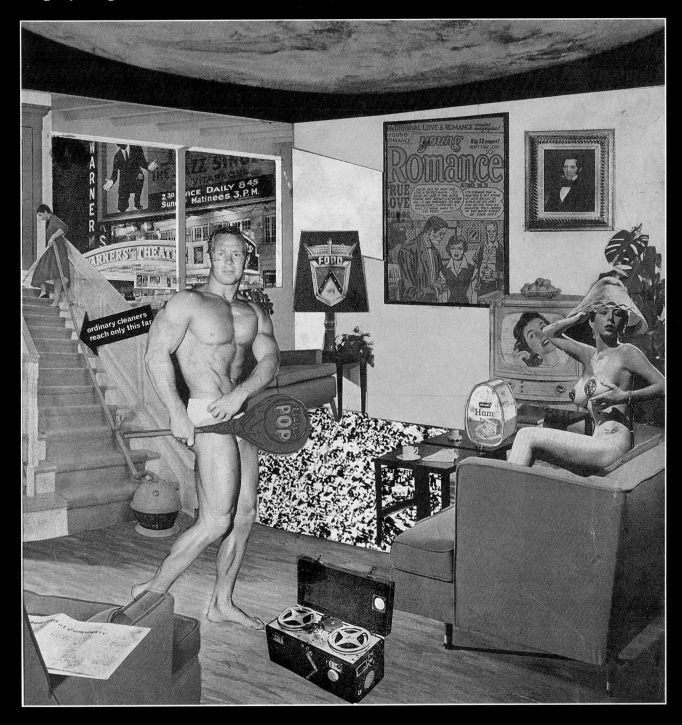

	ART	WORLD EVENTS	DESIGN	THEATRE & FILM	BOOKS & MUSIC
1940	•*Death of Paul Klee*	•*World War II: Italy declares war on Allies*	•*U.S.: Raymond Loewy's Lucky Strike design*	•*Chaplin:* The Great Dictator •*First Bugs Bunny cartoon*	•*Ernest Hemingway:* For Whom the Bell Tolls
1941	•*Surrealists A. Breton & Ernst arrive in New York*	•*Japanese attack Pearl Harbor; U.S. enters war*	•*First aerosol spray cans*	•*B. Brecht:* Mother Courage •*Orson Welles:* Citizen Kane	•*Dmitri Shostakovich:* Leningrad Symphony
1942	•*Edward Hopper:* Nighthawks	•*Battle of Midway: Japan's first major defeat*		•*Bergman and Bogart star in* Casablanca	•*Irving Berlin's song "White Christmas"*
1943	•*Mondrian:* Broadway Boogie-Woogie	•*North Africa: German troops surrender to Allies*	•*Brazil: Oscar Niemeyer's church at Pampulha*	•*Rodgers and Hammerstein's* Oklahoma!	•*Jean-Paul Sartre:* Being and Nothingness
1944	•*Bacon:* Three Studies... •*Death of Piet Mondrian*	•*Allies land in France and drive back Germans*		•*Graham and Copland:* Appalachian Spring *(ballet)*	•*Somerset Maugham:* The Razor's Edge
1945	•*Paris: Jean Fautrier's* Hostages *series exhibited*	•*Atom bombs dropped on Japan; World War II ends*	•*U.S.: W. Gropius founds The Architects' Collaborative*	•*Roberto Rossellini:* Rome, Open City	•*Steinbeck:* Cannery Row •*Britten:* Peter Grimes
1946	•*Gyula Košice makes first neon-light sculpture*	•*UN General Assembly holds first meetings*	•*Italy: Vespa scooter designed for Piaggio Co.*	•*Cannes Film Festival opens*	•*William Carlos Williams:* Paterson *(first volume)*
1947	•*Jackson Pollock's first Action Paintings*	•*India and Pakistan gain independence*	•*U.S.: Alvar Aalto's Hall of Residence, MIT*	•*Tennessee Williams:* A Streetcar Named Desire	•*Albert Camus:* The Plague •*The Diary of Anne Frank*
1948	•*Cobra group founded* •*B. Newman:* Onement I	•*S. Africa: apartheid begins* •*State of Israel proclaimed*	•*Transistor invented* •*Frisbee patented*	•*Vittorio De Sica:* The Bicycle Thieves	•*Alan Paton:* Cry the Beloved Country
1949	•*Fontana first punches holes in his canvases*	•*NATO formed*•*East and West Germany formed*	•*U.S.: Johnson's glass home at New Canaan*	•*Arthur Miller:* Death of a Salesman	•*Simone de Beauvoir:* The Second Sex •*Orwell:* 1984
1950	•*Willem de Kooning:* Excavation & Woman I	•*Korean War begins* •*China invades Tibet*	•*U.S.: Mies van der Rohe's Farnsworth House*	•*Kurosawa:* Rashomon •*Anouilh:* The Rehearsal	•*Loesser:* Guys & Dolls •*Neruda:* Canto General
1951	•*Pablo Picasso:* Massacre in Korea	•*Britain: Churchill re-elected as prime minister*	•*London: Royal Festival Hall*	•*Alec Guinness stars in* The Lavender Hill Mob *(Crichton)*	•*J.D. Salinger:* The Catcher in the Rye
1952	•*Jackson Pollock:* Blue Poles, Number II	•*Kenya: Mau Mau revolt begins*	•*Denmark: Arne Jacobsen's Ant Chair*	•*Gary Cooper stars in Fred Zinnemann's* High Noon	•*John Cage's silent 4' 33"* •*E.B. White:* Charlotte's Web
1953	•*Matisse:* The Snail •*Rivers:* Washington...	•*USSR: Death of Stalin; Khrushchev in power*	•*U.S.: Kahn's Yale University Art Gallery*	•*Beckett:* Waiting for Godot •*Miller:* The Crucible	•*Nadine Gordimer:* The Lying Days
1954	•*Japan: Yoshihara founds avant-garde Gutai group*	•*Egypt: Nasser in power as prime minister*	•*Boeing 707* •*Univers typeface*	•*Marlon Brando stars in Kazan's* On the Waterfront	•*J.R.R. Tolkien:* The Lord of the Rings *(first volume)*
1955	•*Johns paints the first of his* Flag *series*	•*Warsaw Pact formed* •*South Africa leaves UN*	•*W. Germany: Ulm Academy for Design*	•*Cary Grant in Hitchcock's* To Catch a Thief	•*Patrick White:* The Tree of Man
1956	•*British Pop Art begins* •*Hamilton:* Just What Is It	•*Suez Crisis in Middle East*	•*IBM logo* •*Sydney Opera House*	•*John Osborne:* Look Back in Anger •*Godzilla released*	•*Elvis Presley's first hit, "Heartbreak Hotel"*
1957	•*Deaths of Brancusi and Rivera*	•*EEC (European Common Market) founded*		•*Bergman:* The Seventh Seal •*Jean Genet:* The Balcony	•*Jack Kerouac:* On the Road •*Bernstein:* West Side Story
1958	•*Mark Rothko asked to do Seagram murals*	•*CND starts anti-bomb protests*	•*New York: Mies van der Rohe's Seagram Building*	•*Harold Pinter:* The Birthday Party	•*Pasternak forced to refuse Nobel Prize for* Dr. Zhivago
1959	•*Rauschenberg completes* Monogram *(from '55)*	•*Cuba: revolution puts Castro in power*	•*New York: Wright's Guggenheim Museum*	•*Marilyn Monroe stars in Wilder's* Some Like it Hot	•*Death of Buddy Holly* •*Motown label launched*

GLOSSARY

abstract art: art that expresses meaning or emotion through shapes and colors.

Action Painting: a type of Abstract Expressionism that stressed the expressiveness of the artist's action or gesture in creating art.

Art Brut: the name given by Jean Dubuffet to art created by people outside the established art world, such as children; Outside Art.

assemblage: the use of found objects to make a work of art. This technique evolved from collage.

avant-garde: having or developing new, bold, or highly experimental concepts, especially in the arts.

biomorphic abstraction: abstract art based on organic, rather than geometric, shapes.

Color Field Painting: a type of Abstract Expressionism that stressed the expressiveness of large areas of color.

Dada: a movement in art and literature that rejected traditional values and emphasized the absurd.

found object: a natural or manufactured object found by an artist and used either in or as a work of art.

gestural: created by an artist's actions or movements.

Holocaust: the mass slaughter of European Jews by the Nazis during World War II.

monochrome: a work of art in a single color.

ready-made: the name given by Marcel Duchamp to manufactured objects he and other artists chose at random and presented as works of art.

representational art: art that portrays subjects as they are seen in the real world; figurative art.

Surrealism: movement stressing the use of dreams and the unconscious to create art.

MORE BOOKS TO READ

40s & 50s: War and Postwar Years. 20th Century Design (series). Helen Jones (Gareth Stevens)

The 1950s. Cultural History of the United States Through the Decades (series). Stuart A. Kallen, editor (Lucent Books)

Abstract Expressionism. World of Art (series). David Anfam (Thames and Hudson)

Alberto Giacometti: Sculptures, Paintings, Drawings. Angela Schneider, editor (Prestel USA)

The American Eye: Eleven Artists of the Twentieth Century. Jan Greenberg and Sandra Jordan (Delacorte Press)

David Smith. Modern Masters (series). Karen Wilkin (Abbeville Press)

The Essential Willem De Kooning. The Essential (series). Catherine Morris and Willem De Kooning (Andrews McMeel)

Jackson Pollock. Ellen G. Landau (Abradale Press)

Jasper Johns. Michael Crichton (Harry N. Abrams)

Lucio Fontana. Sarah Whitfield and Susan Ferieger Brades (University of California Press)

Mark Rothko. Jeffrey Weiss, John Gage, Carol Mancusi-Ungaro, and Barbara Novak (Yale University Press)

WEB SITES

The Artchive.
www.artchive.com

Francis Bacon Image Gallery.
www.francis-bacon.cx

National Gallery of Art.
www.nga.gov

WebMuseum: Jackson Pollock.
www.ibiblio.org/wm/paint/author/pollock

Due to the dynamic nature of the Internet, some web sites stay current longer than others. To find additional web sites, use a reliable search engine with one or more of the following keywords: *Abstract Expressionism, abstract art, art history, art museums, Color Field Painting, modern art, sculpture, Surrealism,* and the names of individual artists.

INDEX